CREATURES ALL AROUND US

Catch Me If You Can

by D. M. Souza

Carolrhoda Books, Inc./Minneapolis

Library of Congress Cataloging-in-Publication Data

Souza, D. M. (Dorothy M.)
    Catch me if you can / by D. M. Souza.
        p.   cm.
    Includes index.
    Summary: Describes the physicial characteristics, habitat, and life cycle of lizards.
    ISBN 0-87614-713-9
    1. Lizards—Juvenile literature. [1. Lizards.] I. Title.
QL666.L2S697   1992
597.95—dc20   91-37860
                                                   CIP
                                                    AC

RC 52

Manufactured in the United States of America

1 2 3 4 5 6 7 8 9 10 01 00 99 98 97 96 95 94 93 92

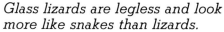

Glass lizards are legless and look more like snakes than lizards.

Catch Me
If You Can

One is 10 feet long, weighs 300 pounds, and has claws longer than a leopard's. Another is legless, looks like an earthworm, and spends most of its time underground. Both are lizards.

No other group of reptiles contains such a variety of members. The glass lizard, for example, is sometimes called a glass snake. This is because it has no legs, and its tail is almost twice as long as its body. When it moves, it wriggles like a serpent.

Geckos are expert climbers.

The gecko, on the other hand, is an expert climber. Most geckos have special pads on their feet, and these pads are covered with millions of tiny hooks. These hooks help the lizards cling to surfaces as smooth as glass. Some geckos can even walk upside down on ceilings.

While lizards cannot fly, as their ancestors once did, the "flying dragon" of Southeast Asia comes close. It has folds of skin along its sides. When it leaps from branch to branch, these folds open like a parachute, and the reptile sails through the air.

Many lizards live and hunt near water. Basilisks can run so fast across water that they don't even sink. The marine iguanas of the Galapagos Islands frequently dive in search of seaweed or other plants.

The majority of lizards, however, are **terrestrial** (tur-RES-tree-uhl), that is, they live on land. They climb up and down trees or bushes or race along fences. Collared lizards can even raise the front of their bodies and run on their hind legs. Their long tails help them keep their balance. Race runners can run very fast. If they didn't have to go too far, these lizards could probably run faster than some people.

A western collared lizard pauses on a rock. Collared lizards can run on their hind legs.

Opposite page: *The Texas horned lizard (above) and the short-horned lizard (below) have sharp scales all over their bodies.*

All lizards are closely related to snakes. Both make up the reptile group known as Squamata. That's the Latin word for "scaly," and that's what both lizards and snakes are.

The lizards known as skinks are covered with smooth, shieldlike scales. Horned lizards have rough, spiny scales. Some legless lizards that live in Florida and California have skin that is folded into rings around their bodies. When they move forward underground, they push these folds against the earth and leave tube-like tunnels behind them.

Some lizards have many rows of scales on the undersides of their bodies. From time to time, they shed patches of their skin, as many reptiles do. The faster a lizard grows, the more often it sheds its skin.

A young five-lined skink warms itself in the sun.

Unlike snakes, most lizards have eyelids that open and close, and ear openings that help them hear. Most also have four legs, five toes or claws on each foot, and a long tail.

Like other reptiles, lizards are cold-blooded, or **ectothermic** (ek-tuh-THUR-mik). Their bodies do not stay at or near a constant temperature, as ours do. They go up or down with the temperature of their surroundings. Lizards keep warm or cool by moving back and forth from sunny to shady places. During cold spells, they hide under logs, leaves, earth, or sand.

About 3,000 different species (SPEE-sheez), or kinds, of lizards live in the warm areas of the world. Close to 350 are found in North America. Maybe you've seen one sitting on a fence, climbing a wall, or doing push-ups on a rock.

8

Green anoles, such as this one, usually turn brown while they bask in the sun.

Show-Offs

Have you ever noticed how some people's faces turn red when they get angry or embarrassed? Well, one kind of lizard, known as an anole (uh-NOH-lee), changes color, too. But its skin doesn't just turn red. It turns green, yellow, pink, and even orange. Let's watch a few anoles in action.

A male green anole shows its dewlap as a warning to another male.

Perched on the limb of a tree is a male green anole. At the moment, it is brownish gray. It is about 6 inches long, and most of its length is in its tail. Covering its body are tiny scales, and hanging from its neck is a loose flap of skin called a **dewlap**. Female anoles do not have dewlaps.

A second male anole arrives on a lower branch. The first one sees him and prepares to signal that this tree is his territory. He fans his dewlap and it turns red-orange in the sunlight. Next, his body appears bright green, and he bobs his head up and down.

The newcomer is not frightened off. Instead, he climbs higher in the tree and faces the other anole. Both open their mouths wide, flap their dewlaps, and bob their heads. The two lizards dart at one another, then twist and turn from side to side. After several minutes, the intruder gives up. He turns a dull yellow and leaves. Meanwhile the winner of the contest struts around in a bright green coat.

Two male green anoles fight each other. Anoles can change color very quickly.

The green anole on the right is beginning to turn brown.

The anole has special cells beneath its **epidermis** (ep-uh-DUR-mis), or outer layer of skin. They contain a substance called pigment that gives the skin color. When the anole is frightened, excited, or sick, the pigment flows upward, and the epidermis changes color. Temperature, sunlight, and shade can also cause changes to appear in the color of the anole's skin.

*Notice the bright blue
patches on this male
fence lizard's side.*

Other lizards flash special
colors when they are excited,
but none looks quite as showy
as the anole. Male fence
lizards, for example, have
bright blue patches on their
sides. Some have blue or
black pouches under their
throats that can grow larger
and make the lizard appear
threatening.

13

An eastern collared lizard strikes a threatening pose.

Even male lizards that cannot change colors have ways of frightening enemies. Banded geckos arch their backs as high as possible. They raise their tails and circle an intruder, bumping it whenever they can. A few geckos even hiss or make strange sounds.

Other lizards try to appear threatening by arching their necks or jiggling crests on their heads or backs. They dance or walk around doing a stiff-legged strut. Many do a number of push-ups on the ground.

During mating season, females are the only ones allowed to enter the male's territory. When a female appears, the male begins to show off. He bobs his head and struts around. If the female allows him to come near, he may rub her chin or scratch her side before mating. After they mate, the female leaves the area.

This female green anole lizard has just laid her eggs.

Little Lizards

A few weeks after mating, a female fence lizard digs a 3-inch hole in soft earth on the sunny side of a hill. Here she lays 10 small white, leathery eggs and covers them with about 2 inches of soil. She then leaves. Like most lizards, she will never return to check on the eggs or to see if they have hatched.

Slowly each egg grows larger and turns from white to a dull gray. In 8 to 10 weeks, the young are ready to hatch. To break out of their shells, they use a tiny tooth fastened to the tip of their snouts. This egg tooth, as it is called, falls off a few days later.

The young are only half the size of their parents and are a little darker in color. During the day they hunt for insects or sun themselves on logs, rocks, or fences. At night they hide under loose bark, between rocks, or under the soil.

Most female lizards lay between 1 and 30 eggs each year under loose soil, rotting logs, or leaves, or even in the open. Lizards that do this are **oviparous** (oh-VIP-uh-ruhs), that is, they lay eggs that hatch outside their bodies.

Not all females abandon their eggs the way fence lizards do. Glass lizards coil their bodies around their eggs. Five-lined skinks stand guard and defend them against predators. Some lizards watch over their eggs from the time they are laid until they hatch. They turn them regularly and care for them much as a mother hen does. A few species of skinks even help their young break out of their shells.

Most female lizards abandon their eggs after laying them, but many female skinks guard their eggs before they hatch.

This baby fence lizard will be ready to mate when it is about a year old.

Other female lizards are **viviparous** (vih-VIP-uh-ruhs), that is, they give birth to live young. The female yucca night lizard, for example, gives birth to one or two live young. So do some horned lizards and alligator lizards.

The young, or **embryo** (EM-bree-oh), developing within its mother's body, is covered with a tough skin, or membrane. When the lizard's day of birth arrives, the membrane breaks, and the young slip out of their mother's body.

Lizards that are born or hatched late in the year usually stay hidden until the following spring, when the weather warms. By then many are old enough to mate and begin laying eggs of their own.

Sharp-shooters

A race runner prepares to hunt for prey.

As the ground warms under the rays of the morning sun, a five-lined skink moves out from its burrow. Its slender brown body is marked by five stripes, and its long tail thins near the end.

The lizard moves slowly at first, then more quickly. Every now and then, its forked tongue touches two holes in the roof of its mouth. These holes are called the **Jacobson's organ**. Each hole is filled with nerves that help the lizard smell what is nearby.

20

Several ants appear along the ground, and in an instant they are zapped by the skink's tongue. A cricket lands close by, and with lightning speed, the lizard nabs it in its jaws. It chews and grinds the cricket with its sharp teeth until the food disappears.

Tongues play an important part in helping lizards catch and hold on to insects. Horned lizards, for example, hold their bodies perfectly still and shoot their tongues out in front of them. When they snap them back, they have several ants stuck on the end. Insects have a hard time escaping quick or sticky tongues.

A six-lined race runner devours its insect prey.

Most lizards are **carnivorous** (kar-NIH-vuh-ruhs), which means that they eat meat. They dine on insects and their larvae, spiders, and earthworms. They swallow small prey whole, but chew larger ones.

A number of lizards eat both meat and plants, so they are said to be **omnivorous** (ahm-NIH-vuh-ruhs). Some lizards are **herbivorous** (er-BIH-vuh-ruhs), that is, they eat only plants. Chuckwallas, for example, feed mainly on the flowers and fruits of cacti.

Most lizards, including this five-lined skink, are carnivorous. Insects are among their favorite foods.

A collared lizard climbs on the back of a chuckwalla. Collared lizards have a powerful bite and often eat other lizards.

There are also lizards that eat other lizards. They are called **cannibals**. The big-headed collared lizard jumps from rock to rock after other lizards. Leopard lizards hide in the shade and wait for small lizards to dart by.

Unlike snakes, which drink by sucking in water, some lizards lap it up with their tongues. Many get water from the juicy insects they eat. Others, such as horned lizards, take drops of water from plant leaves.

This young five-lined skink has just dropped part of its tail.

Gone in a Wink

Two young foxes wrestle in the tall grass outside their den. They tumble and roll against a small rock and push it to one side. A frightened skink dashes out from under the rock and slips past the nose of one of the foxes. With a slap of its furry paw, the fox tries to catch the bright blue-tailed lizard. But in a wink, the skink slithers away, leaving the end of its body wriggling under the fox's paw.

Speed, protective coloring, and clever tricks help many lizards escape danger. But perhaps their best trick is their ability to leave their tails behind them. If you have ever tried catching a lizard by its tail, you know what usually happens.

Many lizards' tails are specially made to break off. When pulled, cut, or bitten, the bones in the tail come apart, the muscles separate, and the skin tears. After the glass lizard loses its long tail, it looks as if its body has been cut in half.

These eastern glass lizards have newly-grown tail tips.

This does not harm the lizard, and there is little or no bleeding when this happens. While the lizard escapes, its tail squirms on the ground or wriggles between your fingers. In a short time, a new tail grows back, though it is never quite as long as the first one. Sometimes, if a tail falls off only partway, a second one grows next to it. Once, someone found a lizard with five tails growing side by side.

Some lizards that cannot shed their tails use other ways of escaping predators. The chuckwalla has skin that hangs on its body like a baggy coat. If its enemy the roadrunner comes near, the lizard slips between two rocks. It takes extra air into its body and blows itself up like a balloon. Try as it will, the roadrunner cannot pull or peck the chuckwalla out from its hiding place.

27

Horned lizards look so much like the desert floors where they live that they are rarely spotted. But some types of horned lizards have a special way of protecting themselves. Along the backs of their heads are rows of long, sharp spines that look like horns. If a hungry snake comes too near, a horned lizard will face its enemy, raise its spines, and take aim. If this threat doesn't work, the lizard will squirt blood out of the corner of its eye. This does not harm the snake but does startle it, allowing the lizard to escape.

Other lizards try to frighten away predators by hissing, snapping, or even biting. The spiny-backed armadillo lizard of South Africa has a special defense. It sticks its tail into its mouth and rolls up like a wreath. Its enemy looks around, and when it cannot find the spiny-back, it finally moves away.

Gila monsters are covered with beadlike scales.

Desert Monster

Evening arrives, and as the hot, dry earth cools slightly, a mouse scampers out of its hiding place. Close by, an 18-inch-long lizard drags itself from under a rock. Its short, stubby legs move slowly. Its coal-black body is splashed with orange. It is covered with scales that look like beads. This is a Gila (HEE-lah) monster, the only poisonous lizard in the United States.

The reptile tracks the mouse with its black, forked tongue darting in and out of its mouth. Unaware of danger, the mouse stops. In an instant, it is caught by a pair of powerful jaws.

As the Gila monster begins grinding its jaws from side to side, poison flows from two glands in its lower jaw. The poison, or **venom** (VEH-num), runs through the lizard's grooved teeth and into the mouse's body. In minutes the mouse is dead.

After finishing its meal, the Gila monster searches for more food. It catches several insects and uncovers a nest of snake eggs. Before the night is over, it also finds some newly laid quail eggs. It breaks the shells, laps up the contents with its forked tongue, then tips its head back to let the liquid run down its throat.

A Gila monster devours a quail egg.

31

Each evening for a week, the Gila monster has been
eating more than usual, and its tail has become very thick.
Like other lizards, it uses its tail as a storage place for
extra fat. This will nourish it when food becomes scarce.
With enough fat stored in its tail, the lizard can survive
for months without food. Gila monsters do not shed their
tails as other lizards do.

The Gila monster's best defense is its bite. If you tease
or excite one, it will turn quickly, hiss, and snap like a
dog. Its bite is similar to that of a snapping turtle. Even
if someone cuts off the lizard's head during an attack, it
will not release its hold. Fortunately for everyone, most
of the time Gila monsters would rather flee than attack.

Sun Watchers

Fence lizards, like most lizards, are active during the day, when temperatures are warmer.

A young girl sprinkles a garden plot where she has just planted sunflower seeds. As the water seeps into the ground, a small lizard scampers out of its hiding place. It is wet and cold, and it rushes to find a patch of sunlight. For several minutes, it sits still, trying to dry and warm itself.

When its body temperature comes close to that of the air around it, the lizard moves on. A moth on a nearby leaf flutters its wings, and in a flash the lizard catches it. The lizard gulps down the moth, then darts here and there looking for other tasty treats in the garden.

During the night, most lizards hide under a few inches of soil to escape the cool temperatures of evening. Sometimes they sleep beneath bark or under a fallen log or rock. Those that are active during the warm parts of the day are called **diurnal** (DY-ur-nuhl).

A few lizards are **nocturnal** (NAHK-tur-nuhl), that is, they sleep during the day and move around at night. Most of these lizards live where nights are warm. The gecko is an example of a nocturnal lizard.

The banded gecko is active at night.

All lizards, whether diurnal or nocturnal, are very sensitive to cold. When winter arrives, they must find warm places to **hibernate,** or spend the winter. These may be 6 to 8 inches under the soil, or in rock crevices. There they fall into a trance. They are not really asleep or unconscious, but they don't act the way they usually do. They do not eat, their breathing slows, and if you poke one, it will barely move. The farther north lizards live, the longer they remain this way.

This Great Plains skink was found hibernating in a burrow under a rock.

All Chihuahua whip-tail lizards, including this one, are female.

Lizards that live where winters are warm usually stay active year round.

People are always making new discoveries about lizards. Not long ago, a group of scientists discovered 13 species of whiptails that were all females. Even though these lizards did not mate with males, they were able to lay eggs that hatched into young whiptails. Scientists are still studying these lizards and their activities.

The next time you see a lizard racing along a fence, swimming through tall grass, or climbing a tree, stop and watch it for a while. You too may make an exciting discovery about one of these lively reptiles.

Scientists who study animals group them together according to their similarities and differences. Animals that have certain features in common are placed in the same group. Lizards belong to the order, or group, of reptiles known as Squamata, and so do snakes. Within the order there are many different families. Two lizard families, Iguanidae and Scincidae, include the lizards most often seen in North America. Below are some of the members of these and other families of lizards, along with a few facts about them.

FAMILY	EXAMPLES	SIZE IN INCHES	FAVORITE FOODS	WHERE FOUND IN THE U.S.
Iguanidae	collared lizards	8-14	insects, spiders, lizards	southwestern states
	fence lizards	3-9	insects, spiders	many areas
	horned lizards	2-7	insects, especially ants	western states
Gekkonidae	geckos	2-6	insects, spiders	Florida and southeastern states
Anguidae	glass lizard	24-42	insects, snails, earthworms, spiders	various areas
Helodermatidae	Gila monster	12-24	small mammals birds' eggs, reptiles	southwestern states
Scincidae	skinks	5-16	insects, spiders, snails, earthworms	various areas

Glossary

cannibals: animals that eat their own kind

carnivorous: able to eat a diet of meat

dermis: the inner layer of an animal's skin

dewlap: a loose fold of skin hanging under an animal's neck

diurnal: active during the daytime

ectothermic: having a body temperature that changes depending on the temperature of the environment

embryo: the young of an animal in the beginning stages of development

epidermis: the outer layer of an animal's skin

herbivorous: able to eat a diet of plants

hibernate: to spend the winter in a hiding place, in a sleeplike state

Jacobson's organ: an organ that certain animals have that helps them smell and taste

nocturnal: active at night

omnivorous: able to eat a diet of both meat and plants

oviparous: giving birth by laying eggs

predator: an animal that hunts and eats other animals

prey: animals that are killed and eaten by other animals

terrestrial: living on land

venom: poison that is produced in the body of an animal

viviparous: giving birth to live young

Index

The photographs are reproduced through the courtesy of: pp. 1 (left), 8, 9, 13, 19, 34, © John Serrao; pp. 1 (right), 10, 11, 15, 23, 25, 30, back cover, © J. H. Robinson; pp. 3, 5, 14, 17, 18, 20, 22, 24, Allen Blake Sheldon; pp. 4, 12, Dwight R. Kuhn; pp. 7 (both), 27, 29, 31, 33, 35, 37, © Joe McDonald; p. 21, © Barney Oldfield; p. 36, © Dan Nedrelo; front cover, © John Peslak. Lizard illustration courtesy of Darren Erickson.